Get Noticed
&
GET HIRED

Action Steps, Strategies and Resources
to Become Empowered & Employed

STEVE MATTER

- Be self-assured, positive and prepared for your interview

- Learn the different personality styles of managers

- Set the stage to become a MVE — a Most Valuable Employee™

- Question yourself whether you are ready to go into business yourself versus returning to the corporate world

- Rebuild your confidence, attitude and belief in yourself

- Help you stand out in a sea of applicants

Read it, apply it, and start on the path back to the workforce.

Aspecial thank you to my friend, Bruce Wright, for helping me look at my world through a larger lens. He has always had the ability for not just seeing the big picture, but the biggest picture of how to bring value to your professional and personal life. It was his insistence that I had a book in me that, ultimately, motivated me to write this one. I hope this book helps the readers look at their own lives through a larger lens and, consequently, be inspired and motivated to take action to attain the job and life of their dreams.

To my family for their love and support which has made me a better son, husband, dad and papa.

Contents

"When the going gets tough, the tough get going."

— Joseph P. Kennedy, Sr. —

The above quote by President John F. Kennedy's father has been one I've thought of many times in my life as I faced hard decisions both personally and professionally. And, as the saying goes, it's not how many times you get knocked down; it's how many times you get back up.

Going through a period of unemployment can test the endurance level of almost anyone. It can create a series of ups and downs, including emotional, physical and spiritual. However, for most people, losing their job is just one aspect of unemployment. For many, it's also about losing their identity, their self-worth, self-confidence and sense of security. It can also be a time of feeling helpless, hopeless and victimized. Often, they feel they have failed their families.

All of these feelings are normal for those who have just lost their jobs. However, there is a way back into the workplace, but it requires resolve, hard work, preparation, practice, time and a support team.

I've been fortunate to spend the majority of my career in senior management roles with financial services companies, where I've interviewed hundreds of people and reviewed tons of resumes. I've found there are three types of people in this world — those who make things happen, those who watch things happen, and those who wonder what happened. In early 2009, I was laid off for the first time in my career and learned firsthand the difficulties of searching for a new job during this Great Recession. Unemployment put me on an emotional roller coaster that I never expected.

Today, millions of people are still looking for work and some economists say the number is higher than government reports, because many people have given up searching for full-time work or are working part-time. A recent article reported that the Federal Reserve predicts unemployment will not show much improvement for the next few years[1], and it's not uncommon to see TV reports about people who have sent out hundreds of resumes without getting a single interview. Others may have been fortunate enough to get interviews, but they haven't been selected for employment. Competition is fierce in this job environment, yet many people go to interviews without proper preparation.

This book is dedicated to those of you who are out of work, to help you turn your anger and frustration into a plan of action to get back into the workforce. My goal is to help empower you to find work or create work by providing ideas, tools and resources. It will also help anyone who is trying to

1Fed Sees high Unemployment All Next Year; Newser, 11/2/2011; http://www.newser.com/story/132437/fed-sees-high-unemployment-all-next-year.html

enter the job market for the first time.

I will share with you my experience as a hiring manager, the guidance and help I received while I was unemployed, and some things I could have done differently. The Action Steps and Recommended Readings will help you to stand out in a sea of applicants by providing you with the tools to improve your probability of employment. The sooner you commit your energies to your job search, the greater your chances of success to Get Noticed and Get Hired.

◆◆◆

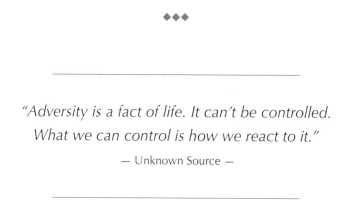

"Adversity is a fact of life. It can't be controlled.
What we can control is how we react to it."

— Unknown Source —

Chapter **1**

I Need To See You

Displaced. That is the latest "corporate speak" for layoffs. Also known as reduction in force, manpower reduction, downsizing or reduction in head count. "We need to reduce your department by 'X' number of heads," was often the discussion prior to a round of layoffs. I have been through it many times during my career. Most of the time it was a reflection of the economy, a time when many firms felt the need to tighten control over expenses to improve financial performance.

I hated going through layoffs. It was a gut-wrenching process to know my actions were going to disrupt people's livelihood and their lives. My prior firm offered a severance package and outplacement help to our displaced employees, but that was small consolation for the emotional turmoil and uncertainty of the future to those impacted. Unfortunately, after several years of being one of the decision makers of who would be laid off, I would find out how it felt to be on the list instead of making it.

In most firms, notifications of layoffs are one-on-one, with supervisors being called on to deliver the bad news. Other firms might call groups of employees into a meeting room to tell them all at the same time that they are losing their jobs. And, it's not uncommon for the now ex-employees to be escorted out of the building after getting the news. Firms are nervous that disgruntled employees may do some kind of damage before leaving. To eliminate that potential, they box up their personal items and mail them to their homes. It's the beginning of the emotional roller coaster.

Termination by Telephone

I found out my "call" was coming by accident. It was Tuesday after Thanksgiving in 2008. The economy was in the toilet, and we had already faced two rounds of layoffs in the first and third quarters. I was on vacation and received a call from my assistant. "Sorry to bother you, but this is important," she said. She then explained that Mark, our branch manager had called to tell her that he just got off a conference call about the layoffs scheduled for Friday. "Our names were on the list," she said. "Is he sure?" I asked. "One hundred percent!" she replied

We both had been with the firm for more than 20 years. The anger and shock came quickly. "When are they supposed to notify us officially?" I asked. "He didn't know, but I guess the call will be from John," she replied. "That jerk," I thought. John was the national sales manager and my boss. I hired him about 10 years ago and supported his promotion. Why didn't he have the courtesy to call and tell me himself?

We had been through a few "fast track" managers that didn't know anything about our business, and we had worked with them to help them understand our business model. "I'm going to call John and find out what's going on. I'll call you back," I told her.

I reached him a few minutes later. "Hey, what the hell is this?" I demanded. "I hear that I'm being laid off." Then I relayed what my assistant had just told me. John replied, "I don't know anything about it." "That's bull," I said. "When I was the national sales manager, I was part of the process and knew everyone who was selected for layoffs." There was a slight pause and he said, "Maybe I'm on the list, too. Let me call Richard and I'll call you back." Richard was our director.

At first I thought this was a good sign. If John hadn't heard anything then maybe I'm okay. Then I started thinking about his relationship with Richard. They never seemed to have gotten along at our management team meetings. I was one of four divisional managers on the team, and at one of our meetings Richard asked John what he wanted him to do at our upcoming sales producer conference. John replied, "I want you to show up and shut up." Then they stared at each other for a few seconds; we could feel the tension.

A few months later we were wrapping up a meeting in Atlanta and, as Richard got ready to leave, he shook hands with John. It looked like a version of Indian wrestling you did as a kid. The kind where you stand foot to foot and try to push your opponent back. After Richard left the room, we told John that it wasn't a good long-term strategy to not get along with your boss. He brushed us off.

About 30 minutes later, John called me back. "Richard just fired me!" he exclaimed. "I tracked him down, told him what you had heard and he said, 'I'll call you back in 10 minutes.' When he returned my call he had a Human Resources Department person on the line. Thirty seconds later I was let go and left on the line with HR." Finishing, he said, "Richard is going to call you and our other managers later today."

Joining the Ranks of the Unemployed

I was at lunch with my wife and daughter when I got the call. I didn't have much of an appetite knowing what was coming. I'm sure I was in a state of shock. My mind kept drifting off. "How could this be happening to me? What could I have done differently to still be on the team?" I was brought back to the present when my cell phone rang. The caller ID displayed the director's phone number. I went out to the parking lot to take the call.

"I need to see you," Richard said. "What is your schedule this Friday? Can we meet in your office at 7 a.m.?" I replied, "Sure, I can make that. What's up?" He replied, "I'll go over it with you in person." I said, "Ok, I'll see you then." We hung up.

In addition to losing my job, I would also lose a pension bonus I would have received had I been allowed to stay with the firm for six more years.

Richard knew I was aware of the circumstances but didn't say anything. He was following the protocol from HR. In my anger I thought, "Okay, I'll let him fly across the country for the Friday meeting, but I'll clean out my office on Thursday and let him show up to an empty office."

It was a tough afternoon as I faced the reality of the situation. How could I explain to my family that, after 21 years with the firm, I would no longer be a part of it? In addition to losing my job, I would also lose a pension bonus I would have received had I been allowed to stay with the firm for six more years.

At around 3 p.m. my cell phone buzzed again. It

was Richard. He said, "I think you know why I want to see you, don't you?" I replied, "Yeah, you are calling me to tell me the rumors are false and I'm still on your team." He said, "I'm afraid that's not correct. Will you be available in the next 10 minutes? I need to call you back." "Sure," I said. We hung up.

I knew what was next. Richard would call back with the HR person on the line. It was the same process I had initiated many times before when I had to deliver similar news to other people.

My phone rang within two minutes. "I have HR on the line with us. We're making some changes to our organization going forward and, unfortunately, you aren't included in our plans. Your position has been eliminated." Three sentences and my career was over after 21 years with this firm. I asked Richard why I was chosen. Of course, I knew he couldn't answer that. He said I could call him the following week after all the announcements were out. I knew he would never tell me. HR wouldn't allow him to say anything that could be used to file a lawsuit on my behalf.

I called my assistant, told her what had happened and said they would be calling her next. We hung up, and then the numbness started to set in. My former assistant, Margaret, is a terrific person and a great employee. When the director called her the next day he opened with, "How are you today?" She replied, "Horrible! I know why you are calling." Richard knew she was aware. It was not a very classy way to handle the end of someone's career.

An Emotional Upheaval

It was official. I had become part of the growing numbers of unemployed in our country, in what was being referred to as The Great Recession. That was three years ago and, today, the unemployed are angrier than ever. Groups of protesters are gathering worldwide in "Occupy Movements" to complain about the economy, lack of jobs, the government gridlock to job creation and what they view as corporate injustice. I now understand their anger and emotions. However, the sooner these protestors can channel their emotions into productive job searches, the greater their chances will be to return to the workforce as employees or to start their own business. Although some of them are peaceful, others have destroyed property and have been arrested. Try explaining that to a prospective employer after a background search.

◆◆◆

"The difficulties of life are intended to make us better, not bitter."

— Unknown Source —

> *"It is during our darkest moments we must focus to see the light."*
>
> — M. Kathleen Casey —

Chapter **2**

Coping with the Emotional Roller Coaster of Unemployment

HOW 3 F'S EQUAL AN "A"

Almost all industries, at all levels, experience cutbacks during difficult economic times — large and small firms alike. And, unfortunately, loyalty and achievement have little bearing in the decision-making process. For example, my neighbor recently lost his job. He worked for a small company in the office equipment industry. He brought corporate know-how to a "Mom and Pop" shop that was struggling to maintain their market share against their mega competitors. One day they told him, "Things aren't working out." He was let go on the same day he had closed the second part of a major government contract, effectively doubling the firm's revenues. Needless to say, he was shocked by how unappreciative the firm was of his contributions.

Being laid off feels the same for most of us. We feel our contributions are not valued or they are overlooked when deciding who will stay with the company and who will be terminated.

> I felt like I was on an emotional and intellectual roller coaster. At first there was shock and denial. "How could they do this to me?"

When I was laid off, I was optimistic. It shouldn't take me long to get back into the workforce. I had worked in my industry for more than 30 years, had a solid reputation for building successful sales teams, and I had a broad base of vendor and peer contacts throughout the country. It was early 2009, and layoffs were happening all over the country, in almost every industry and service. I was in denial that being laid off would really impact me. Because of my contacts, I thought I would be employed within a couple of months. However, it became a full-time job of searching, networking and interviewing to get back into the workforce.

At times I felt like I was on an emotional and intellectual roller coaster. At first there was shock and denial. "How could they do this to me?" I had been a loyal and productive team member. I felt as though part of my identity had been taken from me. I never realized how difficult it would be to say to friends and potential employers, "I *used* to be the ... at my company."

However, I soon learned that what had happened in the past didn't matter anymore. I needed to direct my attention on the future and not let this situation keep me from concentrating on the job search ahead. My head started to spin with questions. Who can I call? What companies will want to talk to me? Who would want someone with my background? I'm near retirement age, will that be held against me? Like many of the unemployed in the 50-plus age group, I had a few interviews where the interviewer tried to find out my age by asking what they thought were "clever" but illegal questions. It was the first time I felt the impact of age discrimination.

During the initial days of my layoff, I experienced a whole gamut of emotions: anger, fear, doubt, denial, stress, frustration, and embarrassment. There were many restless nights when I couldn't sleep. I would wake up in the middle of the night wondering what I should do next, or why did this happen to me in the first place. I felt like an emotional zombie, and found myself succumbing to a "pity party." The emotional toll washed over family members as well. Worried, my wife would ask me, "Will we be okay?"

Most Americans live paycheck to paycheck, and surveys show that very few working families have enough savings to cover their expenses for more than three months. I was fortunate to have a severance package to help us get by for about one year. I knew I had to become focused and stay positive. I needed help to stay on track, stay active and to get my support team in order. I needed to align myself with positive individuals who believed in my capabilities and in me.

HOW 3 Fs EQUAL AN "A"

As you begin your journey of re-employment, you will need a strong support structure. I like to call this your *"3 Fs"* — *Faith, Family and Friends.* By tapping into this support system, you are better able to maintain a positive *Attitude* and to stay on course as you implement your job search. Your belief or faith, whether spiritual or in yourself, can be a driving force to help you maintain a positive mind-set on this journey.

The Bible tells us we will go through many tests during our lifetime, and being unemployed can be one of the most stressful tests we endure. One of the passages that helped me stay focused is from James 1:3.

"When your faith is tested, your endurance has a chance to grow. So let it grow, for when your endurance is fully developed you will be strong in character and ready for anything."

Prayer and meditation can help provide clarity in thought and give you the mental strength to keep a positive frame of mind. When things became overwhelming for me, I would remember to P.U.S.H. — Pray Until Something Happens.

You also need to have faith in yourself. Write down the attributes that make you a great employee. Include examples of your strengths and how you incorporated them into your previous jobs. Writing these down will help you articulate them during the interview process and will help build your self-confidence. Don't get stuck on pity or the bitterness of your situation. People like being around, and are more likely to hire positive people.

When I was on my high school football team, our coach would read us a poem at the beginning of each season about keeping a positive outlook. This message has stuck with me throughout the years.

The Man Who Thinks He Can[1]

If you think you are beaten, you are,

If you think you dare not, you don't

If you like to win, but you think you can't,

It's almost a cinch you won't.

If you think you'll lose, you're lost

For out in the world we find,

Success begins with a fellow's will;

It's all in the state of mind.

1 Walter D. Wintle, "The Man Who Thinks He Can."—Poems That Live Forever, comp. Hazel Felleman, p. 310 (1965).

If you think you're outclassed, you are;

You've got to think high to rise,

You've got to be sure of yourself before

You can ever win a prize.

Life's battles don't always go

To the stronger or faster man;

But soon or late the man who wins

Is the one WHO THINKS HE CAN!

— Walter D. Wintle —

A Positive Attitude

Ray, a former employee of mine, was one of those individuals who was always upbeat. He was a sales leader year in and year out, no matter what the economic conditions may be. When I asked him what his "secret" to success was, he told me he always kept a positive attitude, even if there were circumstances in his life that were challenging. Whenever someone asked him how business was, his answer was always, "Awesome! Business is great. People need our products and services now more than ever. Let's review some of your clients." People gravitated to Ray because he was always positive and prepared with ideas to help his advisors and their clients.

Your family can be your rock of strength to get you through these tough times. My wife was my biggest cheerleader. She constantly reminded me of my accomplishments and that she knew a job was on the horizon. She encouraged me to remain optimistic.

More than likely, your family will encourage you with their love and support throughout your job-seeking process. Your close friends will also help sustain you. Just remember, it is important to constantly reach out to people for their support during this time. Without it, you may start to lose confidence in yourself and begin to feel hopeless.

However, even if you strive to maintain a bright outlook, there will be times when negative thoughts creep into your mind. Thoughts such as: How much longer is this going to go on? Why didn't the recruiter call me back? What will I do if my money runs out? Can I hold on to my house? Will we still be able to retire?

Unfortunately, there isn't a switch you can throw to automatically stay upbeat during your time of unemployment. This is why you need to talk to someone each day who can be a positive influence on your attitude. Have gratitude for having your faith, family and friends in your life as you press forward to find your new job.

◆◆◆

*"Never give up. Keep your thoughts and
your mind always on the goal."*

— Tom Bradley —

ACTION PLAN #1

1. Although it may be difficult emotionally, you need to notify the important people in your life about your situation as soon as possible. The sooner they know, the quicker they can lend their support and help you with your search.

2. Write down your attributes and skill sets in a descriptive paragraph, as a mini resume. Think of this descriptive paragraph as your *Magnetic Message™* to draw jobs to you. Email this information to friends and family as you notify them about your situation. Ask them to reach out to others with your personally written description of your skills and background.

3. You often find out who your *real* friends are during this time.

> *"False friends are like our shadow,*
> *keeping close to us while we walk*
> *in the sunshine, but leaving us the*
> *instant we cross into the shade. "*
>
> — Christian Nevell Bovee —

Chapter 3

Friend or Faux?

During your working life you probably cultivated many relationships, many of them business related — colleagues, vendors, union reps, association members or industry contacts. During your association with them, you probably began to feel they were your good friends. However, soon after being laid off, you may have found that those you considered to be friends really weren't.

After I was laid off, Bob, a retired friend of mine, called and invited me to lunch. He had been laid off during his career and offered to share his own experiences with me. One of the first things he said to me was, "You will soon learn who your real friends are. Be prepared to be shocked by those you consider to be close colleagues and associates. They'll act as though you never existed." He explained that he and others he had talked to had experienced this, and I should expect the same.

I respected Bob's opinion, but I was having a hard time thinking any of my "friends" would do this. After all, most of my business contacts acted like my team was crucial to their firm. We often dined together, and they sponsored our training sessions and participated in company meetings. They made me feel as though our business relationship was better than any of those they had with other firms.

However, Bob's words soon came true. Before long it became evident who was a true friend, and who wasn't. I had a contact list of colleagues, wholesalers, vendors and other business connections I had cultivated over the years. After being out of work for two weeks, I prioritized my list, placing my best relationships at the top. Then I started emailing and calling them.

My messages were short and to the point. After all, there was no need to leave a long, detailed message; they knew me and would be willing to help because we had such a great relationship, right? Boy was I wrong! Many people whom I had considered to be good friends did not bother to call back or to respond to my emails. Apparently, they weren't true friends. Fortunately, many friends did respond and I received several leads for interviews, one that eventually led to my current position.

It was very enlightening to discover who my real friends were. Several of the people who didn't return my calls and emails are vendors or resources to my current firm. Of course, my relationship with them isn't as warm and fuzzy as before. I've spoken with other people who were laid off and they all experienced this same issue by varying degrees.

However, don't be dissuaded. Reaching out to friends and contacts during this time is crucial to the networking process. Asking for job referrals and favorable introductions is the old-fashioned way of networking. Most often the best jobs aren't placed on websites or in employment ads, they are found through personal networking. The point of reaching out to friends, vendors and colleagues is to cast as wide of a net as possible for employment opportunities. Social media sites such as Twitter, LinkedIn® and Facebook® are also great mediums for connecting with people.

> It was very enlightening to discover who my real friends were. Several of the people who didn't return my calls and emails were vendors ...

As I mentioned before, there were things I did then that I would now do differently. I believe I could have increased the response from business contacts by providing details about my plans to stay in the industry and to continue working with them — similar to this sample email.

Jim,

You may have heard that I was laid off last week by XYZ Co. As you can imagine, I'm very disappointed with their decision and have started my search to find a similar position with another firm. I'd like to schedule a short call with you to get your opinion of some of the firms I'm considering contacting.

Part of the success of our department at XYZ Co was due to the partnership we had with you and your firm. I expect that we will continue to work together once I'm employed again.

I can be reached at 555-555-5555 or Steve@mymail. com

I sincerely appreciate our friendship/partnership that we've developed over the years and look forward to continuing it at my new firm.

Steve

A communication like this does several things. It lets people know:

- You plan to stay in the same industry.

- You have a list of companies you're considering that they may already have a working relationship with, and that you may end up working together again.

- No matter where you land, you would like to work with them again. This could provide a new opportunity for their firm.

- You respect their opinion.

- After reaching out like this, if they don't respond it could damage a future working relationship with you.

Networking with people in your industry can be the key to getting the job you want, and referrals from people you know and have worked with can put you ahead of others seeking the same position.

◆◆◆

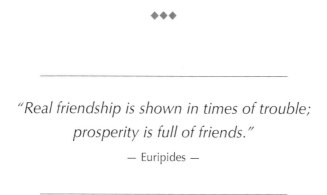

"Real friendship is shown in times of trouble; prosperity is full of friends."

— Euripides —

ACTION PLAN #2

1. Create a contact list of colleagues, vendors, union contacts, association members, etc. *Then, change business acquaintances into friends with influence.*

2. Get to know key centers of influence in your business such as union officials and association board members.

3. List 5 Centers of Influence for your occupation:

    _____

    _____

    _____

    _____

    _____

4. Join online associations to increase contacts in your line of business.

5. Create an email and phone message (script) that includes everything you want to convey to your contacts to get a helpful response.

6. Ask your external contacts about firms similar to yours. What companies would they recommend as prospective employers?

> *"Acceptance of what has happened is the first step to overcoming the consequences of any misfortune."*
>
> — William James —

Chapter 4

It's Not "AA" but It Feels Like It

How to Get Your Game Plan Together

The group appointment was at 9 a.m. Forty of us quietly filed into the windowless room, taking our seats randomly. Many had a vacant look in their eyes. A few seemed to know each other. We were all there to start the healing process and prepare to get our lives back in order.

Our leader introduced herself and provided an overview of what the next few weeks would be like. Then she asked us to state our names and former occupations. Some introductions seemed more painful than others. Some were embarrassed, some were angry, and we all wanted help.

> The outplacement firm was a critical component for providing a structure that would prepare us for the challenges ahead.

"Hi, I'm Dave and I used to be the finance manager for a local car dealership." "I'm Marcia and I was an administration assistant at a software company." The introductions continued until all 40 of us had described our former employment identities, which included all sorts of businesses, industries and occupations. It was difficult for many of the attendees, and it reminded me of a movie scene when a person at an Alcoholics Anonymous (AA) meeting first stands up to acknowledge his or her struggle with alcohol. The only difference was, our struggle was to get our act together and find a new job. Just like an AA meeting, every session started with individual introductions. It proved to be therapeutic over time.

We were in an outplacement program. Fortunately, our former companies included it as part of our severance package. There are several outplacement firms in the country that are either employer-sponsored or available to individuals for a fee.

It was an employment boot camp for the newly displaced, and over the next few weeks we attended classes to help us in our employment search. We prepared resumes, role-played interview scenarios and, in short, learned how to build a business plan that would help get us back to work. The outplacement firm was a critical component for providing a structure that would prepare us for the challenges ahead.

With so many people unemployed you need to take advantage of every program available that can give you the edge over your competitors.

The first step at our outplacement center was a Career Assessment program. We needed to decide if we wanted to stay in the same industry, move into another field or start our own business. If we wanted to work in another field, we needed to determine what additional education or experience would be required. If we were leaning toward self-employment, was it the right time to start our own business? Or, would we be better off going back into the corporate marketplace?

Career assessment exams can be taken at most community colleges and online. Once you've decided what position you want or if, instead, you want to start your own business, your process begins!

One of the first things we were told was that the fastest way to a new job was with a referral. Obviously, there are many job sites on the Internet that can be helpful, but a personal referral is the quickest way to get an interview. It's much better than giving a corporate recruiter another unknown resume.

We were advised to get business cards for use in networking opportunities. Our cards needed to include our desired position and skill sets. Here is an example of my business card:

Front side:

Steve Matter

Senior Sales Leadership/Manager

Recruiting/Training/Coaching High Performance Teams

949-555-5555   Steve@mymail.com

Back side:

Areas of expertise include:

- Internal and external team leadership
- Estate Planning
- Interdepartmental cross-selling
- P&L responsibility
- Sophisticated insurance solutions
- Managing through cultural changes

The key words and backside bullet points came from my resume summary.

Our leader suggested we set up a new email account exclusively for our job search, one that was accessible from any computer or smartphone such as Hotmail®, Yahoo®, Gmail™ or AOL®.

We also spent a lot of time on networking. We learned to use social networking sites such as Facebook, LinkedIn and Twitter, and we spent lots of hours developing our personal network the old-fashioned way, by defining who our centers of influence were. Time was also devoted to using Internet job sites, such as www.Indeed.com. Indeed.com actually helped some of my colleagues find jobs. We also searched for specific industry jobs by entering key words such as "construction job" in search engines, such as Google™ or Yahoo®.

Outplacement firms have numerous connections to employers and can help you with proactive job development.

Building a resume took longer than I expected. I found it wasn't such a simple process, if done correctly. My resume was refined several times before it met the approval of my outplacement mentor. It had been years since I had to assemble a resume, and the "rules" of order had changed. We were told that a recruiter spends about 30 seconds reviewing a resume to decide if the applicant has the background for further consideration.

To help the recruiter or interviewer access this information quickly, skill sets and accomplishments need to be featured in the Career Summary section at the top of the resume. They don't want to search to determine why they should hire someone; instead, this information should be easy to find. Remember, a resume has one purpose: to get you noticed for an interview.

If you have been sending out a lot of resumes without getting a response, you need to have it reassessed and changed. Obviously, it isn't making the impact you need to get you an interview. Also, your resume should be tailored for each job opportunity you are seeking. People who send the identical one for every job opening they are applying for are not maximizing their opportunity to stand out. There are many professional resume services available to re-write your resume for a fee. If you are in this situation, it may be money well spent.

Many outplacement firms provide office space and the use of computers to give you a workplace environment in which to make calls. This alleviates unnecessary background noise when you are networking or talking to prospective employers. Outplacement firms also provide critical coaching and can help you build a step-by-step plan to assist you in transitioning to your next job.

You need to be persistent in your job search. Getting a job in a field in which you have little or no experience can be hard. You also may find that certain jobs require special licenses or other types of certifications. To increase your chances of being hired, educate yourself about the job requirements before applying, to make sure it is a good fit for you.

◆◆◆

*"Knowledge becomes wisdom
only after it has been put to practical use."*
— Unknown Source —

ACTION PLAN #3

1. If your firm hasn't provided you with outplacement support, use your search engine to look up outplacement firms. Some are employer-paid only. If you can't afford an outplacement firm or are new to the job market, follow the steps below to help in your search.

2. Order business cards and set up a new email address for all job search correspondence. Print a list of bullet points of your skill sets and attributes on the back of your business card.

3. Refine your resume for each job opportunity.

4. Practice interview questions and responses.

5. Join LinkedIn.com and other business-related websites.

6. Sample of job search sites:
   - Monster.com
   - Careerbuilder.com
   - TheLadders.com
   - Findtherightjob.com
   - Indeed.com
   - Simplyhired.com
   - Linkedin.com

> *"Achievement is preceded by preparation, courageous action and faith that success is inevitable."*
>
> — Bruce Raymond Wright —

Chapter 5

How to Make Your Resume Stand Out

30 Seconds for Impact

Imagine yourself at an interview and the interviewer says, "Thanks for meeting with me today. You have 30 seconds to impress me with your skill set and background." This is essentially what your resume has to do to get you through the first phase of the employment search gauntlet. You've probably heard the saying that you only get one chance to make a first impression; this applies to your resume as well!

The introductory section of your resume must have impact for the recruiter to recognize that you have the qualifications required for the position available. A tight summary of skills and areas of expertise need to be included in the Career Summary section at the top of your resume. Think of this section as your Magnetic Message™. You need to use it to attract prospective employers, by listing your applicable skills and attributes that will get you noticed for an interview.

Having a hard time deciding on the right words to include? Just think about your desired position. What are the qualities and experience you can bring to that position? Or, imagine one of your centers of influence is meeting with a business owner or manager who needs someone with your background and experience. What would you want them to say about you that describes you in the most positive way, and will make him or her want to meet with you? That is the message you need to convey in your Career Summary section.

Here is my resume Career Summary:

> *Senior Sales Manager with extensive regional and national experience leading insurance professionals in the area of Wealth Management. Successful track record in recruiting, training and coaching high-performance teams. Well-developed communication and strategic thinking skills with the ability to resolve difficult situations.*

Areas of expertise include:

- *Internal and external team leadership*
- *Interdepartmental cross-selling*
- *Sophisticated insurance solutions*
- *Estate planning*
- *P & L responsibility*
- *Managing through cultural changes*

My Career Summary is posted on my LinkedIn page and continues to draw interest from recruiters. I also used the key words and areas of expertise bullet points on the back of my "job search" business card.

Although it is not a "cast in stone" rule, most of the outplacement specialists I met with encouraged me to have a one-page resume. Remember the 30-second rule! No one wants to read a long resume, especially if they have dozens and maybe even hundreds to review. It used to be common practice to start a resume with a Job Objective paragraph. However, today most counselors will tell you that using a Job Objective paragraph is passé in this job market. Employers know your objective is to get hired, that's why you applied. Instead, they want to know what you bring to the table that makes you the right candidate for the position. That's why your resume needs to have the Career Summary at the top.

If you find a job posting you feel is suitable for you, analyze the description and requirements, looking for key words and skills you can use in your resume to ensure it contains information that can be directly linked to that position. Did you know that large corporations often use key-word software to analyze resumes that are uploaded into the HR database? Thoroughly reading the job description and including those key words will increase your chance of being called in for an interview.

This is an actual job description posting from an Internet job site:

> *Payroll Supervisor to process payroll for 1000+ employees on a weekly basis using the ADP Enterprise System and ADP Report Writer. This position is also responsible for posting to the general ledger, journal entries and month end close for payroll. Strong software and process improvement skills are a must. This role also requires excellent attention to detail, problem solving skills and advanced Microsoft Excel including V lookups and Pivot Tables.*

I'm sure lots of applicants will be uploading their resumes for this position. And, fortunately, the listing provides a lot of key words that can be used in the Career Summary of the resume. Most likely this firm uses a software program to search resumes for key words to match the job description, or the interviewer will be looking for these attributes/skills when reviewing the resumes. Let's assume that this job description fits you perfectly, and you have the skill sets described above. After making sure your wording is in alignment with the job description, your resume Career Summary might look like this:

> *Energetic, self-motivated payroll supervision professional with a passion for all software and processing systems. Proven leader in coaching, building and mentoring team members to achieve outstanding on-time deliverables for all payroll requirements including general ledger postings, journal entries and payroll deadlines. Well-developed communication and strategic-thinking skills with the ability to resolve difficult situations.*
>
> *Areas of Expertise Include:*
>
> * *ADP Enterprise System*
> * *Advanced Excel Skills*
> * *Software analysis*
> * *ADP Report Writer*
> * *V lookups and Pivot Tables*

This Career Summary covers most of the key words in the job posting.

The rest of your resume should list previous positions you have held and provide additional bullet points of your accomplishments and achievements at these positions to back up your Career Summary. If you find another job description with different requirements, you will need to change your resume to be in alignment with the key words and skill requirements of that opportunity. Of course, it's also important that they match your actual experience.

Make sure you list only areas of expertise that you actually can demonstrate, and don't blow your credibility during the interview by overstating your qualifications. Firms are looking for employees to add value to their organization. Strive to be a Most Valuable Employee.™

Quantify your achievements and use power phrasing when writing your descriptions. For example instead of writing:

Managed a 15-person sales team in a 10-state territory.

You might write:

Directed/Coached 15 high-performance sales profes-sionals across a 10-state territory that exceeded goals by 25% over the past two years.

You can find examples of power phrasing on many of the resume-building websites.

Have your resume printed on quality paper — nothing colorful. Let your Magnetic Message™ Career Summary grab their attention, not some horribly colored paper.

There are some things you definitely do not want to put into your resume, including:

- Age or marital status. I recently reviewed a resume that stated the person was recently divorced and that's why they needed a job.

- Weaknesses. One applicant included "horrible handwriting" as their weakness. That question may not come up, don't volunteer irrelevant information.

- Personal interests. One applicant listed "dreaming" as a personal interest! Personal interests have no bearing on your job and could eliminate you as a candidate if you list something like dreaming!

- Oldest jobs listed first. Recruiters don't like reading your career history in reverse.

Follow the example on page 38 to craft a magnetic resume to get you noticed and called for an interview.

Students entering the job market should emphasize the following on their resumes:

- Summary of why you are a viable candidate. A description of what you bring to the position.

- Education

- Relevant classes to the position

- Qualifications for the position

- Computer skills (if applicable)

- Pre-professional experience

- Organizations

Your Name

City

Phone • Email Address

Career Summary:

Magnetic Message™ paragraph: *(This includes your skill sets and expertise. Use parts of this paragraph as bullet points on the back of your business card.)*

Professional Experience: *(List in chronological order, putting the most current employer first.)*

Company name, city, time frame (i.e. 2003 – 2011)

Your title and job responsibilities:

- Achievement #1 in this role

- Achievement #2 in this role

- Achievement #3 in this role

- Achievement #4 in this role

Repeat relevant firms and positions *(You don't need to list early jobs that have no bearing on the position you are seeking.)*

Education: *(List colleges, tech schools or highest level of education achieved.)*

Licenses and Professional Development:

List relevant licenses or courses pertaining to the position

References Available Upon Request *(No need to provide these until they ask for them.)*

- Awards

- Presentations

- Research projects

- Internships

- Volunteer work

- Activities that demonstrated leadership

Some counselors advocate including a cover letter with your resume; however, I am not a fan of cover letters. As an interviewer, I never read them prior to reviewing resumes. If the candidate's qualifications warranted an interview, I wanted the individual to articulate points during the interview that usually would be included in the cover letter.

How to Maximize a Job Fair

You may have seen news reports on TV about people handing out hundreds of resumes at job fairs without getting any results. Here are some tips on how you can improve your experience.

Obviously your Career Summary cannot be in complete alignment with every job description at the job fair. Collect job descriptions for the jobs you find most appealing and best fit your qualifications. If specific descriptions are not available, ask for the job number so you can look them up on the company website. When you get home review each one and adjust your resume to include any relevant experience or skill set missing in your Career Summary, then resend your resume to the firm. A customized resume for a specific job will help increase your chances of being called in for the interview.

Procrastination is the Enemy of Preparation

Don't wait until the last minute to throw your resume together, or to look up the employer's address just before the appointment. When you make a decision to do something, put it into action without delay. It's one thing to decide to do something, and it's entirely another thing to actually do it. I'm sure that's why the Nike slogan is "Just Do It" instead of "Just Decide"!

New Year's resolutions are great examples of decision versus action. Each year millions of people resolve to make changes in their lives — lose weight, exercise more, stop smoking, be a better parent or spouse. And, while they make a conscious decision to do these things, we all know from personal experience that actually doing them rarely happens, if at all.

If you are unemployed you have had change thrust upon you. You need to take action. Often the unemployed find themselves outside their comfort zone as they try to get back into the workplace. Often, they find it to be difficult, yet are not willing to change their approach. One of my favorite definitions of insanity is doing the same thing over and over again, and expecting different results. If your resume isn't resulting in interviews, or your networking efforts aren't paying off, change them. Your resume is not "a one size fits all" document. It needs to change, as job descriptions for the same type of position can vary from company to company and can have different requirements. For each position, you need to modify your resume by customizing the skills and experience in your Career Summary to get noticed!

"Today's preparation determines tomorrow's achievement."

— Unknown Source —

ACTION PLAN #4

1. Work on your Magnetic Message™ and use it as a framework for the Career Summary section of your resume.

2. Use your Internet search engine to look up "resume tips." There are many free websites that provide alternative resume formats, action words, design ideas and resume reviews.

3. Try to limit your resume to one page in length.

4. Print your resume on quality paper, no colors.

5. If possible, before sending your resume get a spe-

cific job description from the prospective employer to help match your skills and expertise to the job requirements in your Career Summary.

6. The job of your resume is to get you an interview. While it is your "foot in the door," your interview will determine whether or not you get the job.

"Luck is what happens when preparation meets opportunity."

— Seneca, Roman Philosopher,
1st Century AD —

Chapter **6**

Preparing for Your Interview and the "5-P Rule"

Hope, as they say, is not a strategy. You should be preparing for an interview long before you have one scheduled on your calendar. Remember the old saying, "How do you get to Carnegie Hall? Practice, Practice, Practice." The same is true for interview preparation. To paraphrase Yogi Berra, "Preparation is 90% mental, the other half is physical."

THE "5-P RULE"
Proper Preparation Prevents Poor Performance

You are in a fierce competition to become employed, and you will soon find that every winner has an "edge." The majority of the time that edge is preparation. Look at professional athletes. Many have been playing the same sport for most of their lives. Yet every year when their season begins, they go through the fundamentals of training again. They know that practice will make their responses second nature. When famed Green Bay Packers coach Vince Lombardi started spring training each year, he would hold a football in his hands and say, "Gentlemen, this is a football." It was reviewing the basics — the repetition — that led to the Packers being the dominating NFL team in the 1960s. Remember, the key to a well-prepared interview is practice, practice, practice. The result of practice is a natural, non-robotic, execution of your attributes, skill sets and experiences during the interview.

Over the years, I have interviewed hundreds of job applicants, and it has always amazed me that some candidates would come in unprepared or dressed like they were on a weekend leisure trip. One time I was working for a firm that had a strict business attire policy that required suits. One job candidate arrived dressed in casual slacks and an open-collared shirt. He introduced himself to me and said, "So what do you have for me?" I replied, "I have nothing for you. You have wasted your time and mine." Remember, you only get one chance to make a first impression. Make it count. This person should have inquired about the dress code and come prepared for a professional interview.

Another time I was in Hawaii interviewing a prospective sales candidate. The dress code is very relaxed in Hawaii; Aloha shirts and slacks are the standard business attire in the islands. The interview was not going in the direction I had thought it would. He talked mostly about himself and did not ask many questions about our structure, or about the opportunities the job provided. At the end of the meeting, as a courtesy, I asked him for his business card. He looked me straight in the eye and with complete sincerity said, "My face is my business card." I burst out laughing. Not professional and not hired.

> It is imperative you research the company you will be meeting with before your interview.

It is imperative that you research the company you will be meeting with before your interview. One of the most common questions you will be asked is, "What do you know about our firm?" It is not impressive to say, "I don't know anything about your company." Search the Internet to gather as much information as you can about the prospective employer. Anything you can learn about the company, its history and its culture will play to your advantage.

Go to every interview with the attitude that you will be the "star" candidate. You want to knock them over with your preparation and skills. Think of the interview as your audition, an opportunity to shine more than any other candidate.

When it is Your Turn to Shine, Be Brilliant!

Not every company will be the right fit for you. However, you should not cross a firm off your list of potentials just because the job doesn't seem ideal for you. I'm a big proponent of going to as many interviews as possible, if the firm is in the industry you have chosen. Of course, there will be positions that you may not consider to be your ideal job. However, by doing the interview you may discover there are other positions available that become open to you because you met with their recruiter/interviewer and blew them away with your skills, experience and professional preparation.

An additional benefit to having multiple interviews is that you get to practice your interviewing skills in a live situation. They may ask you questions you hadn't anticipated that will help you prepare for your next interview. Consider each interview an opportunity to fine-tune your skills.

Many interviewers will run through your job history asking you what you liked and disliked about each position and why you left the firm. Preparing for these questions will help you respond without hesitation. Don't appear to be searching for answers during your interview, as it is a dead give-away that you are unprepared.

Inevitably you will be asked, "What do you consider to be your greatest strengths?" Don't just regurgitate what you have written on your resume; instead, talk about the attributes that make you a valued employee. Employers want to hire people they perceive will add value to their organization. They want individuals who can become MVEs – Most Valuable Employees™. We will talk more about the MVE in Chapter 8.

My current employer puts new hires through a testing program to evaluate their strengths. Our firm believes it is better to focus on building a person's strengths rather than trying to change a weakness into a strength. I wish I had taken a similar test during my period of unemployment. It would have helped me articulate my strengths during interviews.

For example, let's say two of your strengths are "achievement" and "being responsible," and your resume reflects these strengths without stating them precisely. When asked what your strengths are, you might respond:

"As you can see from my resume, I've been an achiever throughout my career. I've been promoted several times and have had responsibilities added to my job duties, because I've demonstrated that I can be relied on to meet or exceed goals. I also like to build a team environment where the group excels instead of just a few individuals. Coaching and mentoring my team members has played an important role in my success.

However, you may get the reverse question, "What is your greatest weakness or weaknesses?" This is a tough question unless you've thought it through ahead of time. I like to modify it with my answer. My answer wouldn't work if I was looking for an IT job or accounting position. I like to say:

"I believe everyone has areas in which they can improve. One of the areas I'd like to improve in is my computer spreadsheet skills and PowerPoint presentations. I've recently taken some classes to improve my skills in this area."

> Incorporate parts of your Magnetic Message™ summary into the key job points that have been discussed during the interview.

It's important to name a weakness/area of improvement and tell them what you are doing to increase your competency. Whatever you say, avoid the cliché, "I work too much" or "I'm a workaholic,"

They may also ask you this question, "Why should we hire you for this position?" Or, "Why do you want to work for our firm?" You should have prepared a 60-second "commercial" of why they should hire you. Memorize and practice saying it so it flows naturally. Don't be caught searching for an answer to this important question. Incorporate parts of your *Mag-*

netic Message™ summary and then tie it into the key job points that have been discussed during the interview.

If, like me, you are over the age of 50, it is easy to feel that you are the recipient of age discrimination. You may encounter an interviewer who asks inappropriate age-related questions. One interviewer asked me, "What year did you graduate from college?" Another asked, "How old are your children?" My response was, "Is this relevant to the position I'm applying for?" Both interviewers danced around my question. One said he wanted to know a little more about me. Bull! If the interviewer is asking inappropriate and illegal questions and could end up being your manager, I say PASS. This is a strong signal as to their character and integrity. Life is too short to work for jerks, especially at our age!

If possible, ask a friend or family member to help you do a mock interview and record it. Provide them with questions you might hear during an interview — questions about previous employers, length of employment, and why you left. Dress as though you are at the interview. Often, people are surprised at how they look when the video is replayed. How is your posture? Do you appear friendly? Are you smiling or serious? Are your answers/explanations flowing smoothly? Are you robotic? Do you look interested or desperate?

If you use a camera phone to videotape your "interview," connect it to a computer or TV for viewing so you can get a better perspective of your performance. If you don't have access to a video recorder, practice in front of a mirror.

When it's time for your actual interview, tell yourself it will be as easy as A, B, C:

ATTITUDE – It will be positive because you're prepared, you have researched the job and rehearsed your responses.

BELIEVE – You believe in yourself. You have the skill sets and experience for the job.

CONFIDENCE – Your self-assurance will be evident when you articulate your qualifications during the job interview.

You also should prepare questions for your interviewer. Not having questions to ask him or her shows a lack of preparation. Some sample questions include:

- Who is the best employee you have in this position now?

- What is it that makes them stand out?

- Will I be able to spend some time with them if I'm selected for this position?

- What's your long-term vision for your company?

- How have you weathered this economic environment?

- What is your policy for advancement and pay raises?

- How will my performance be measured?

- Describe the culture of your firm.

- Is there anything in my resume that would prevent me from being a final candidate for this job?

- What are the next steps in your process to fill this position?

People who ask astute questions of the interviewer are perceived as being confident and capable. Their interest in knowing what makes the company successful and how they can contribute to its future success is appreciated. It's an excellent way to wrap up an already great interview.

Ultimately it will be your interview that will determine if you are hired. Several factors will come in to play:

- Your willingness and desire to prepare for the best possible interview experience.

- Your work history, skills and experience for the position.

- Your ability to connect with the interviewer and to demonstrate that you are the best candidate for the job.

◆◆◆

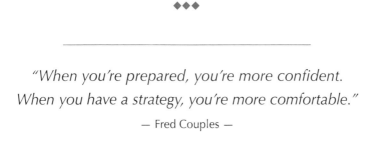

"When you're prepared, you're more confident. When you have a strategy, you're more comfortable."

— Fred Couples —

ACTION PLAN #5

Once you confirm an interview date, create a "to do" list for each interview:

1. Request a formal job description if one is available.

2. Ask how much time is allotted for the interview and if there will be time allotted for you to ask questions.

3. Confirm the address and map it on Yahoo Maps or MapQuest to ensure you have enough time to get to the interview *early*. If possible, make a dry run a day or two in advance of your interview date to the location. It's best to do it during the time of day your interview will take place.

4. Ask for the names, titles and departments of the people you will be meeting.

5. Google the company to gain as much information as possible.

6. Recruiters will often ask what you know about their firm to see if you had the initiative to investigate the company.

7. Good recruiters will provide you with detailed background information on the company, the position and your interviewers.

8. Make a list of interview questions you anticipate the interviewer will ask you.

9. Role-play the interview with a family member or friend.

10. If possible, video record your practice session to view your posture and "body English," as well as your responses.

11. Prepare the questions you will ask the interviewers.

12. Take a pad of paper and pen to your interviews to have your questions available and to write pertinent notes during the interview.

13. Wear the proper attire for your interview. If you are interviewing for an office position, ask if the attire is business or business casual.

14. Send a thank-you card or email to the interviewer as soon as the interview is over.

15. You are prepared and rehearsed to make a great impression!

Recommended Reading:
StrengthsFinder 2.0 by Tom Rath

> *"The task of the leader is to get his*
> *people from where they are to*
> *where they have not been."*
>
> — Henry Kissinger —

Chapter 7

Personality Style of Your New Boss

Attila the Hun to Gandhi

Starting a new job is an interesting process. It's a new environment with new colleagues, procedures and supervision. No matter what they are called — boss, supervisor, manager, foreman or leader, they all come with different personalities, business styles and expectations.

During your lifetime you have probably experienced the styles of many "managers," including parents, teachers and sports coaches. Some managers are supportive and nurturing. Others are dictatorial and intimidating. Some can't seem to make a decision, while others will tell you what you want to hear to avoid conflict. Knowing your new manager's style will go a long way to helping you be productive and enjoy your work environment.

While growing up, we learned how to deal with the different personalities in our lives. I was fortunate to have many positive influences — my parents, teachers, coaches and early managers.

During my college years I worked at Disneyland, known for its culture of always being courteous and positive to fellow "cast members" and the public. However, one of my experiences did not have the typical Disney movie ending. In the early 70s, I had aspirations of joining their management team. I got a management application form from HR, and started filling it out. One of the questions was, 'What is your salary goal?' At the time I was making $5 an hour working at The Golden Horseshoe. I thought about it for a moment and wrote $75,000. I considered that to be a pretty good goal compared to what I was making. After all, why not make it a big goal?

The interviewer started to review my application, then he suddenly stopped and said, "You want to earn $75,000! The president of Disneyland doesn't make that much money!" "I guess I need to look for another opportunity," I replied. Today I wonder what might have happened if I had responded,

"Well then, eventually I'd like to have the job as President of Disneyland." Don't let others squash your goals or dreams.

After graduating from college, I began a sales career and after eight years I became an assistant sales director for a large financial services firm. Jerry, my immediate supervisor, was what I refer to as a "true leader." He was a great coach and mentor, he understood our business model and he strived to build a great team. I was privileged to become a part of his management group.

Shortly after my promotion, the management team met at the home office for the annual kick-off management conference. This was my first Home Office meeting with the other directors of the department. I had envisioned the meeting being held in a large wood-paneled room, complete with a giant oval walnut table and beautiful leather chairs. We would all discuss how we were going build our organization and meet our goals. I expected to see portraits of our firm's leaders on the walls and an amazing view of the ocean from our headquarter's vantage point on the coast.

Boy, was I naïve! We entered a windowless conference room with cheap Formica tabletops shaped in a large square to accommodate 20 of us. The walls were covered with fabric to help with soundproofing, and the flooring was cheap carpet squares that could be replaced if someone spilled coffee. The stackable chairs had hard seats that made your butt go numb after an hour.

For the most part, the management group was comprised of

successful "A" type personalities. Just before the meeting was to start, Charlie, the senior manager of the division, came in. I had never met him. He was an imposing figure — very tall and with a Fu Manchu mustache. I expected to hear a recap of the previous year's results and his vision for the current year. Since this was my first meeting with Charlie, I was eager to observe his leadership style and hear his plans for our future.

Charlie looked around the room and said, "All right you (expletives), I've given you your goals and I don't give a (expletive) how you get there. If you don't make your goals by year-end I'll fire your (expletive)." WHAT? Where was the business etiquette? What about the Rules of Decorum? I'm glad he wasn't looking directly at me because I'm sure my eyes were as wide as saucers. "Welcome to the big leagues of management," I thought to myself.

The others in the room looked intently at Charlie and then one of the directors said to him, "We feel Don [the senior sales director] is a roadblock to us making our goals. We'd like to speak to you without him in the room." Don looked like he had been kicked in the gut. He left the room and a heated discussion ensued regarding his management style and effectiveness. Later, Don returned to give a presentation. You could, as they say, cut the tension with a knife. I felt like I was watching a movie about a business takeover. This was the start of my education on dealing with the different management types that would cross my path during the next 20-plus years. "We're not in Disneyland anymore Toto!" I thought.

Later that year, I was promoted and, consequently, had more one-on-one conversations with Charlie. I learned early on that he was not one for chitchat. His style was results-oriented and direct, and he liked to see if you believed in your position. This led to lively conversations during which my points were contested. He wanted to see if I had conviction and the data to back up my stance. The conversations were never "warm and fuzzy." When I would call, he'd usually say, "What do you want now?" I'd reply that I was calling to make his day. He would usually chuckle and then say, "What is it (expletive)?" When we were done he would say, "Anything else?" "Not at this time," I'd reply. Then he would say, "Go back to sleep."

> His style was results-oriented and direct, and he like to see if you believed in your position ... if I had conviction and the data to back up my stance.

Although Charlie with his intimidator style was tough to deal with at times, he would back you up if you did the right thing ... in his opinion, that is. Once we were in competition for a very large transaction. One of our vendors had received our request on behalf of a potential client and also was representing a competitor for the same client. The vendor promised us we would receive the same terms as our competitor. In the end the vendor reneged, and we lost revenues of more than $100,000. I had kept meticulous notes on the vendor's promises to our firm during the negotiations. A few days later one of the vendor's managers called and offered to pay us $30,000 as a "peace offering." I wanted the entire $100,000. They said I could take the $30,000 or forget it. I said, "Take the $30,000 and shove it!" A few seconds after I hung up the phone I thought, "I bet I don't have the authority to make that decision!"

I called Charlie to share the conversation I had with the vendor. He said, "Let me get this straight. We lost this deal and they offered us $30,000 because they value our account, and you tell them to shove it?" "Yes," I said. "They cheated us, and I have the documentation to prove it." The pause in our conversation seemed to last forever, then he said, "Good for you. I'll have them meet with us next week." We ended up getting more money and, luckily, I still had my job. It was a lesson learned.

I had another manager whose style was similar — without the expletives. He had a nameplate on his desk that simply had "NO" printed on it. When I asked him why it was on his desk, he explained he always said no to requests to see if the person had a conviction about what they were asking. If they didn't push back, he felt they really didn't believe in what they were requesting.

There are numerous resources available that can help you learn about the various personality styles and how to deal with them in order to have the best working relationship possible. Most of the books or articles on this topic address four personality types. The ones I've read are pretty similar in the characteristics of the personality categories, and they are usually put in a quadrant. It's assumed that most individuals will have a dominant category with tendencies toward the other categories.

I have my own quadrant based upon the managers I've encountered over my career. They are:

Attila/Intimidator	True Leader/Coach
The Know-It-All	Gandhi/Peacemaker

Attila/Intimidator (AI)

This person can be very controlling and difficult. When dealing with this personality, they want facts and results. This manager enjoys challenging employees when they present their ideas or requests. Although they like to challenge you, they don't like being asked to justify or explain their rationale for decisions. "Because I said so," is a common response. These intimidator types are often very successful at achieving goals and benchmarks because they are driven to succeed.

You will learn to be very disciplined when working with the AI. If you come to them with a problem, be sure to have a couple of solutions to discuss. When presented with facts, the AI is a quick decision-maker.

The Know-It-All (KIA)

I have worked with a couple of KIAs. One manager I worked with told me it never took him longer than three days to master anything. I knew we were in trouble as soon as that sentence came out of his mouth. This type loves to debate to show off their "superior" intellect and knowledge of the topic at hand. They have a knack for taking a simple task and turning into a long, drawn out, detailed assignment. The KIA then likes to take full credit for the success of the project.

If they don't consider an idea to be theirs, you may find it difficult to get your project or ideas approved by the KIA. It is often best to approach them to seek their opinion, guidance or counsel. Their egos feed on that. Have your facts and solutions available for discussion. Hopefully, they will follow your lead or come to a similar, favorable decision for what you want to accomplish. The KIA loves data. The more data they are provided, the better they can opine on why or why not the issue you brought to them should be approved.

Some KIAs suffer from "paralysis by analysis" when making decisions. This usually delays a result because they feel the information you brought to them was incomplete. I have had some KIAs use "I have insufficient data" as an excuse to postpone a decision they really didn't want to make, but they wouldn't admit it. This technique is called the Muhammad Ali "rope a dope" delay. You keep banging away asking for a decision, and the KIA will ignore you, hoping you will eventually stop asking.

Other KIAs love to teach and share their knowledge with their teams. This can be extremely beneficial when training a team to deliver the KIA's message to other employees or clients. I worked with a KIA like this. It was like going through an MBA program; it was an incredible learning experience. The only downside was this KIA also had Attila/Intimidator tendencies.

Be ready for feedback and constructive criticism with KIAs. Asking for their guidance or opinion will help them view your message in a positive manner and, hopefully, it will help you get the results you want.

Gandhi/Peacemaker (GP)

This manager is usually very friendly and non-threatening. The problem with most GPs is that they will say whatever you want to hear and then will renege at some later date, especially if someone in a more powerful position convinces them that the decision was wrong. They avoid controversy as much as possible, and they hate to make decisions that will create a confrontational issue.

The GP is easy to get along with and will be sympathetic to issues that are used as excuses for underperformance. GPs like to know they can trust you. They are happy as long as you are performing as expected and do not create issues with other employees. This manager is pretty "hands-off" versus a micro-manager.

True Leader/Coach (TLC)

This person is a rare find. You'll find they have several aspects that are similar to the other personality types. However, they use them in constructive ways to build a positive working environment. They have high energy levels and have the instincts to pull people together to utilize their strengths and build a collaborative structure that will benefit their team and the firm.

The TLC "inspects what they expect." That is, they set goals and plan activities and then monitor them to make sure individuals are carrying out their assignments. They want to keep the team on track and will provide coaching and training to increase the team's effectiveness and to keep them from getting stale. They are very motivating and enthusiastic. The TLC will help people see and do what they don't see or understand in themselves.

When a TLC needs to discipline someone, they do it with dignity. They are firm without being condescending or belittling. Working for a TLC is like being on a sports team where everyone will do anything for the success of the team and the coach.

As you can see, knowing your manager's personality and how to approach them will make working in the organization much easier and reduce potential frustrations. Understanding their management approach will help you communicate more effectively with them.

◆◆◆

"The greatest Leaders help others to see and do the extraordinary things they aren't capable of without Leadership."

— Bruce Raymond Wright —

ACTION PLAN #6

Google Personality Styles. You'll find several websites that provide information on the various management styles and how to understand the different personality types. Study them assertively until you have sufficient understanding for them to be of real value to you.

Recommended Reading:
Personal Styles & Effective Performance by David W. Merrill and Roger H. Reid

"Just make up your mind at the very outset that your work is going to stand for quality ... that whatever you do shall bear the hallmark of excellence "

— Orison S. Marden —

Chapter **8**

Become a M.V.E. — Most Valuable Employee

Once you are hired you should strive to become what I call a "MVE" — *Most Valuable Employee™*. A MVE makes every effort to go beyond their normal duties to help the organization with "wins." They look for ways to improve the workplace by making processes more efficient, improving interdepartmental communications and cooperation with relevant departments, etc. In short, they are active employees versus ones who show up, put in their hours and don't contribute anything beyond their written job description. MVE's are those employees who put extra effort into their jobs as a matter of everyday practice. They make things happen in the workplace instead of waiting for something to happen. The employee that is perceived as a MVE has a greater chance of surviving future layoffs.

Early in my career, before I became a manager, I participated once a month on a cable TV show presented by two of our employees. It was broadcast throughout the southern half of California. Clients tuned in for financial reports and to hear about strategies and products. The show provided an 800 number for inquiries about the daily topics. Our office would then receive phone calls from prospective clients who were interested in purchasing these services and products.

> The employee that is perceived as a MVE has a greater chance of surviving future layoffs.

Rather than try to make all the sales myself, I told my manager that I felt it would benefit our region if I shared these leads with my colleagues who were in closer proximity to the prospects. By doing this we could see the clients more quickly, which should result in more sales and create a more positive client experience. Doing this caught the attention of our management team and helped me become an assistant manager. It was a win/win situation for everyone involved.

Once I became a manager, I strived to become a MVE to help not only our department, but also those with whom we interacted on a frequent basis. I started an Advisory Council comprised of our sales representatives. The goal of the council was to have more consistent employee communications with the management team that would lead to better overall performance and job satisfaction. If I saw issues or problems, I made sure I had some solutions to take to my manager to help fix them, instead of just complaining. Make a difference in your job, treat others with respect and always maintain your integrity. It takes a long time to build a good reputation and only a second to ruin it.

Asking employees for input is very empowering for them. It gives them the feeling that their opinions are valued by the company and their positions are vital to its success. Typically, input from the group increases productivity and job satisfaction. It makes them feel like a MVE – a Most Valuable Employee™.

When you join your new firm, start thinking of how you can become a *Most Valuable Employee™*. Figure out how to improve the effectiveness, fulfillment and prosperity of those around you. Then actively make it happen. Help make those around you better and more productive.

◆◆◆

"Welcome the task that makes you go beyond yourself."

— Frank McGee —

Action Plan #7

1. During the first 60-90 days on your new job, make a list of ways you can help your new firm with "wins" and review with your supervisor.

2. Watch for opportunities to help others achieve more.

Chapter 9

Employee or Entrepreneur?

If you are currently unemployed or a first-time job seeker, one question you should ask yourself is, "Do I want to be an employee or in business for myself?" Being self-employed, whether you start your own small business or purchase a franchise, can be tremendously rewarding. However, it comes with many challenges as well.

Being an entrepreneur is not for the weak. You will spend countless hours building, guiding, nurturing, coaching and protecting your business. Being the owner of a business is TOUGH. You will wear all the "hats" that are normally shared in a large business. You are the bookkeeper, marketer, salesperson, administrator, service department, complaint department, benefits department, human resources, etc. If you are tired of working 40 hours a week at your current job, you need to be prepared to work 60-80 hours or more when you run your own business. Additionally, there can be enormous risks, both financially and emotionally. That is why it is important that you love what you do. Most entrepreneurs have a passion for their work. It is one of the key drivers to being in business for yourself — you are doing something you love.

Many people are not cut out to leave the "security" of being an employee, although the word "security "is a very tenuous concept these days. Sometimes the road to self-employment comes from the realization that you have the experience and confidence to be your own boss. A few years ago, my friend Bruce Wright and I were discussing being an entrepreneur with another associate of mine. Bruce told my friend that if he was ready to leave the corporate world that Bruce has contacts and resources for being self-employed that would "rock his world." My associate quickly dismissed the idea saying it was too risky at this stage of his life with funding college for his children and mortgage obligations.

Often people become compartmentalized by their jobs. It becomes hard for them to think "outside the box," as my friend Bruce likes to say. They become defined by their corporate title, and they cannot see potential for anything else.

Sometimes they are so narrowly focused that they cannot see or embrace the greatness that already exists within them. And, because it is invisible to them, they cannot envision the unlimited possibilities that already exist for a bold and more abundant future.

Several years ago Bruce encouraged me to write a book. He said he felt my experiences could help others in the financial services area. At that time I was too focused on my corporate job and could not commit to the project. I made excuses in my mind why I did not have the time to pursue writing.

> Often people become compartmentalized by their jobs. It becomes hard for them to think "outside the box."

Fortunately, being unemployed opened my thinking beyond my corporate existence. Rather than write a financial book, I decided that my journey through unemployment and my experience in interviewing and hiring people for decades could benefit those struggling to get back into the workplace or wanting to start their own business. I started to think outside the box.

Many self-employed people have amassed great wealth working for themselves, instead of corporate America. But being an entrepreneur can be a daunting task filled with risks. Before jumping into entrepreneurship, assemble a team of trusted advisors to review your ideas and help you determine if you have the skill sets, business acumen, capital and resources to successfully launch and sustain your business idea. If you are lacking in any of these resources or characteristics, perhaps you can align yourself with other professionals who have the skills you are missing and assets to help fill in your gaps.

Often a team approach is essential to success in business and life. There is an old adage, "Look before you leap." Be cautious and cover your bases. Make sure you have the time and have identified the resources available to you before going into business for yourself. Compile a group of trusted advisors, such as a banker, CPA, attorney, and financial advisor, and with their help, look with as much clarity as possible at all aspects of business management before making the leap of your life.

◆◆◆

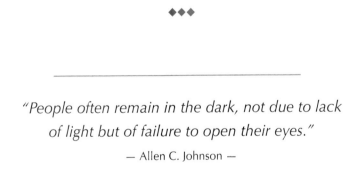

"People often remain in the dark, not due to lack of light but of failure to open their eyes."

— Allen C. Johnson —

Action Plan #8

1. Outline your business idea then create a business plan with the help of your trusted advisors

2. Assemble trusted advisors for input:

   - Business banker

   - CPA

   - Attorney

   - Financial advisor

   - Insurance agent

   - Business mentor

   - Vendors in your business category

Recommended Reading:

Hard Knocks MBA by David W. Miller II

> *"The thing that contributes to anyone's reaching the goal he wants is simple wanting that goal badly enough"*
>
> — Charles E. Wilson —

Chapter **10**

Get Ready, Get Set Get Going!

Going though a period of unemployment is one of the most stressful times an individual and their family will endure. Oftentimes during this period, life does not feel fair and it is easy to feel down. However, the best thing you can do is to continuously channel your energy into getting back into the workplace or starting your own business as quickly as possible. To do this you will need support and a game plan. Like with any game plan, you will need to prepare for contingencies.

Let your family and friends know of your situation as soon as possible. Rely on them and your faith to get you through this difficult time.

Become a networking machine. Many good jobs or business opportunities are not formally posted. Establish a new email address just for your job search. Have business cards made and include bullet points on the backside of your card from your *Magnetic Message*™ Career Summary.

> Let your family and friends know of your situation ... Rely on them and your faith to get you through this difficult time.

If your firm offers outplacement help, utilize every class available and take advantage of every coaching opportunity. If outplacement is not offered or you cannot afford it, utilize the Action Steps in Chapter 4 to build your own outplacement experience.

Write a dynamic opening Career Summary to include on your resume. If your resume is not resulting in interviews, change it. Have your outplacement firm review it, or have friends and family who have interview experience evaluate it.

Practice answering interview questions. Have someone video you if possible. It is amazing to see what we look like on video. Often our body language is not portraying us like we think it is. Have a list of questions for your prospective employer. Be interested in the position and in the company. Be engaging and friendly in the interview. *Look interested and confident ... not scared or desperate.*

> *"Some say that practice makes perfect,*
> *but this is not necessarily so. Perfect*
> *practice sufficiently repeated is a*
> *more certain path to success."*
>
> — Bruce Raymond Wright —

Learn the different personality types. This will help you tremendously in communicating and working with your new manager and in meeting their expectations.

Strive to become a MVE – a *Most Valuable Employee*™. Set a goal to do five or six things at your new job that will benefit the firm. By doing this, you and everyone around you will profit. Perform your job with the same dedication and care as if you were the owner of the business. Doing this will have a positive effect on your attitude, your performance and your job satisfaction.

We spend a large part of our lives at our place of business. Choose a place that you look forward to going every day. Whether you choose to stay in the corporate world or go out on your own, you should feel empowered by your decision if you have made the proper preparations. My friend Bruce advises, "Changing strategies, tactics or tools to achieve your vision is often part of what is necessary to succeed. There is no shame in adjusting yourself into a better alignment with success."

Stay positive; feel empowered by your preparation and ready for opportunity. Then set out boldly, in full faith that your success is inevitable. Put yourself in alignment with success and you will begin to attract new possibilities and opportunities that will enable you to live your life with greater abundance.

"Change your thoughts and you change the world."

— Norman Vincent Peale —

Steve Matter has more than 30 years of experience in national and regional leadership roles at Fortune 500 companies and has a complete picture of the entire employment process. His innovative methods have consistently allowed his employees and divisions to meet or exceed even the highest of standards, benchmarks and quotas. Nevertheless, one day his world was turned upside down.

After 21 years as a highly proficient executive with a proven track record, he was dismissed without regard to his accomplishments. As has happened to other people, he initially went through an emotional roller coaster and then set his mind to finding an even better job.

This book guides you through the logic, emotions, strategies, tactics and tools he used to find a spectacular new position where he is appreciated and empowered to build the success of his regions, while elevating other divisions within his company. The lessons from Steve's 30-plus-year journey give you priceless insights on how YOU can align with, and actually get the kind of job or career you desire. The practical advice contained within this book will speed and ease YOUR journey to get measureable results for a happier and more fulfilling life and career.

Steve and his family currently reside in Southern California. Through his writing, speeches, television and radio interviews, Steve is a driving force dedicated to putting you and all of America back to work in more fulfilling and enriching ways.

◆◆◆